GROWING
in
WISDOM

CONTENTS

✿ ✿ ✿ ✿ ✿ ✿ ✿

INTRODUCTION

HAVE YOU EVER BEEN IN A SEASON OF LIFE WHEN you had more questions than answers? Are you in one of those times right now? Maybe you're waiting on God to fulfill a dream He has placed in your heart . . . you've been hurt and need God's healing touch . . . or maybe you're struggling financially and desperately need a breakthrough. It's in those moments that we need God's wisdom.

THE BIBLE SAYS in James 1:5, *If any of you is deficient in wisdom, let him ask of the giving God [Who gives] to everyone liberally and ungrudgingly, without reproaching or faultfinding, and it will be given him.*

THIS IS SUCH AN AMAZING PROMISE FROM GOD! It assures you that if you are in need of wisdom today, all you have to do is ask and God will give it to you. The only requirement on your part is that you come to Him with a humble, open heart, ready to hear what He has to say to you.

I'M BELIEVING that this booklet of scriptures is one of the ways He will do that. You can receive God's wisdom as you meditate on His Word, allowing His Truth to take root in your heart and impact every area of your life.

WHATEVER YOUR SITUATION IS TODAY, God's wisdom is the key to making right choices and maintaining peace as you do what you need to do. Remember that God loves you and He wants to help you. Seek Him by looking into His Word and you will find everything you need to have the life He has planned for you!

Joyce Meyer

DISCOVERING
who you are in
CHRIST

Do not be conformed to this world (this age), [fashioned after and adapted to its external, superficial customs], but be transformed (changed) by the [entire] renewal of your mind [by its new ideals and its new attitude], so that you may prove [for yourselves] what is the good and acceptable and perfect will of God, even the thing which is good and acceptable and perfect [in His sight for you].

ROMANS 12:2

For we are God's [own] handiwork (His workmanship), recreated in Christ Jesus, [born anew] that we may do those good works which God predestined (planned beforehand) for us [taking paths which He prepared ahead of time], that we should walk in them [living the good life which He prearranged and made ready for us to live].

EPHESIANS 2:10

But you are a chosen race, a royal priesthood, a dedicated nation, [God's] own purchased, special people, that you may set forth the wonderful deeds and display the virtues and perfections of Him Who called you out of darkness into His marvelous light.

1 PETER 2:9

Having gifts (faculties, talents, qualities) that differ according to the grace given us, let us use them: [He whose gift is] prophecy, [let him prophesy] according to the proportion of his faith.

ROMANS 12:6

Once more Jesus addressed the crowd. He said, I am the Light of the world. He who follows Me will not be walking in the dark, but will have the Light which is Life.

JOHN 8:12

LIVING
out your
DREAM

Delight yourself also in the Lord, and He will give you the desires and secret petitions of your heart.

PSALM 37:4

You will show me the path of life; in Your presence is fullness of joy, at Your right hand there are pleasures forevermore.

PSALM 16:11

Now to Him Who, by (in consequence of) the [action of His] power that is at work within us, is able to [carry out His purpose and] do super-abundantly, far over and above all that we [dare] ask or think [infinitely beyond our highest prayers, desires, thoughts, hopes, or dreams].

EPHESIANS 3:20

A man's mind plans his way, but the Lord directs his steps and makes them sure.

PROVERBS 16:9

But, on the contrary, as the Scripture says,
What eye has not seen and ear has not
heard and has not entered into the heart
of man, [all that] God has prepared (made
and keeps ready) for those who love Him
[who hold Him in affectionate reverence,
promptly obeying Him and gratefully
recognizing the benefits He has bestowed].

1 CORINTHIANS 2:9

HaVING a sound MiND

For the rest, brethren, whatever is true, whatever is worthy of reverence and is honorable and seemly, whatever is just, whatever is pure, whatever is lovely and lovable, whatever is kind and winsome and gracious, if there is any virtue and excellence, if there is anything worthy of praise, think on and weigh and take account of these things [fix your minds on them].

PHILIPPIANS 4:8

Set your minds and keep them set on what is above (the higher things), not on the things that are on the earth.

COLOSSIANS 3:2

You will guard him and keep him in perfect and constant peace whose mind [both its inclination and its character] is stayed on You, because he commits himself to You, leans on You, and hopes confidently in You.

ISAIAH 26:3

See to it that no one carries you off as spoil or makes you yourselves captive by his so-called philosophy and intellectualism and vain deceit (idle fancies and plain nonsense), following human tradition (men's ideas of the material rather than the spiritual world), just crude notions following the rudimentary and elemental teachings of the universe and disregarding [the teachings of] Christ (the Messiah).

COLOSSIANS 2:8

Who has known or understood the mind (the counsels and purposes) of the Lord so as to guide and instruct Him and give Him knowledge? But we have the mind of Christ (the Messiah) and do hold the thoughts (feelings and purposes) of His heart.

1 CORINTHIANS 2:16

Lean on, trust in, and be confident in the Lord with all your heart and mind and do not rely on your own insight or understanding.

PROVERBS 3:5

For those who are according to the flesh and are controlled by its unholy desires set their minds on and pursue those things which gratify the flesh, but those who are according to the Spirit and are controlled by the desires of the Spirit set their minds on and seek those things which gratify the [Holy] Spirit.

ROMANS 8:5

HEALTHY, HEALED & WHOLE

A happy heart is good medicine and a cheerful mind works healing, but a broken spirit dries up the bones.

PROVERBS 17:22

He personally bore our sins in His [own] body on the tree [as on an altar and offered Himself on it], that we might die (cease to exist) to sin and live to righteousness. By His wounds you have been healed.

1 PETER 2:24

But He was wounded for our transgressions, He was bruised for our guilt and iniquities; the chastisement [needful to obtain] peace and well-being for us was upon Him, and with the stripes [that wounded] Him we are healed and made whole.

ISAIAH 53:5

Bless (affectionately, gratefully praise) the Lord, O my soul, and forget not [one of] all His benefits—Who forgives [every one of] all your iniquities, Who heals [each one of] all your diseases.

PSALM 103:2-3

My son, attend to my words;
consent and submit to my sayings.
Let them not depart from your
sight; keep them in the center of
your heart. For they are life to
those who find them, healing and
health to all their flesh.

PROVERBS 4:20–22

Be not wise in your own eyes; reverently fear and worship the Lord and turn [entirely] away from evil. It shall be health to your nerves and sinews, and marrow and moistening to your bones.

PROVERBS 3:7–8

Do you not know that your body is the temple (the very sanctuary) of the Holy Spirit Who lives within you, Whom you have received [as a Gift] from God? You are not your own, you were bought with a price [purchased with a preciousness and paid for, made His own]. So then, honor God and bring glory to Him in your body.

1 CORINTHIANS 6:19–20

EXPERIENCING financial PEACE

Bring all the tithes (the whole tenth of your income) into the storehouse, that there may be food in My house, and prove Me now by it, says the Lord of hosts, if I will not open the windows of heaven for you and pour you out a blessing, that there shall not be room enough to receive it.

MALACHI 3:10

And my God will liberally supply (fill to the full) your every need according to His riches in glory in Christ Jesus.

PHILIPPIANS 4:19

But you shall [earnestly] remember the Lord your God, for it is He Who gives you power to get wealth, that He may establish His covenant which He swore to your fathers, as it is this day.

DEUTERONOMY 8:18

A good man leaves an inheritance [of moral stability and goodness] to his children's children, and the wealth of the sinner [finds its way eventually] into the hands of the righteous, for whom it was laid up.

PROVERBS 13:22

And He said to them, Guard yourselves and keep free from all covetousness (the immoderate desire for wealth, the greedy longing to have more); for a man's life does not consist in and is not derived from possessing overflowing abundance or that which is over and above his needs.

LUKE 12:15

RECEIVING God's LOVE

For I am persuaded beyond doubt (am sure) that neither death nor life, nor angels nor principalities, nor things impending and threatening nor things to come, nor powers, nor height nor depth, nor anything else in all creation will be able to separate us from the love of God which is in Christ Jesus our Lord.

ROMANS 8:38–39

I love those who love me, and those who seek me early and diligently shall find me.

PROVERBS 8:17

For the Father Himself [tenderly] loves you because you have loved Me and have believed that I came out from the Father.

JOHN 16:27

Such hope never disappoints or deludes or shames us, for God's love has been poured out in our hearts through the Holy Spirit Who has been given to us.

ROMANS 5:5

For God so greatly loved and dearly prized the world that He [even] gave up His only begotten (unique) Son, so that whoever believes in (trusts in, clings to, relies on) Him shall not perish (come to destruction, be lost) but have eternal (everlasting) life.

JOHN 3:16

But God shows and clearly proves His [own] love for us by the fact that while we were still sinners, Christ (the Messiah, the Anointed One) died for us.

ROMANS 5:8

We love Him, because He first loved us.

1 JOHN 4:19

making good DECISIONS

If any of you is deficient in wisdom, let him ask of the giving God [Who gives] to everyone liberally and ungrudgingly, without reproaching or faultfinding, and it will be given him.

JAMES 1:5

The way of a fool is right in his own eyes, but he who listens to counsel is wise.

PROVERBS 12:15

Apply your mind to instruction and correction and your ears to words of knowledge.

PROVERBS 23:12

Your word is a lamp to my feet and a light to my path.

PSALM 119:105

The reverent and worshipful
fear of the Lord is the beginning
and the principal and choice
part of knowledge [its starting
point and its essence]; but fools
despise skillful and godly Wisdom,
instruction, and discipline.

PROVERBS 1:7

For the Lord gives skillful and godly Wisdom; from His mouth come knowledge and understanding.

PROVERBS 2:6

He who walks [as a companion] with wise men is wise, but he who associates with [self–confident] fools is [a fool himself and] shall smart for it.

PROVERBS 13:20

FREEDOM from FEAR

Be strong, courageous, and firm; fear not nor be in terror before them, for it is the Lord your God Who goes with you; He will not fail you or forsake you.

DEUTERONOMY 31:6

The Lord is my Light and my Salvation— whom shall I fear or dread? The Lord is the Refuge and Stronghold of my life—of who shall I be afraid?

PSALM 27:1

For God did not give us a spirit of timidity (of cowardice, of craven and cringing and fawning fear), but [He has given us a spirit] of power and of love and of calm and well-balanced mind and discipline and self-control.

2 TIMOTHY 1:7

I sought (inquired of) the Lord and required Him [of necessity and on the authority of His Word], and He heard me, and delivered me from all my fears.

PSALM 34:4

What time I am afraid, I will have confidence in and put my trust and reliance in You. By [the help of] God I will praise His word; on God I lean, rely, and confidently put my trust; I will not fear. What can man, who is flesh, do to me?

PSALM 56:3–4

Yes, though I walk through the [deep, sunless] valley of the shadow of death, I will fear or dread no evil, for You are with me; Your rod [to protect] and Your staff [to guide], they comfort me.

PSALM 23:4

It is the Lord Who goes before
you; He will [march] with you;
He will not fail you or let you go
or forsake you; [let there be
no cowardice or flinching, but]
fear not, neither become broken
[in spirit—depressed, dismayed,
and unnerved with alarm].

DEUTERONOMY 31:8

LOVING others

If I speak in the tongues of men or of angels, but do not have love, I am only a resounding gong or a clanging cymbal. If I have the gift of prophecy and can fathom all mysteries and all knowledge, and if I have a faith that can move mountains, but do not have love, I am nothing.

1 CORINTHIANS 13:1–2 (NIV)

Love is patient, love is kind. It does not envy, it does not boast, it is not proud. It does not dishonor others, it is not self-seeking, it is not easily angered, it keeps no record of wrongs. Love does not delight in evil but rejoices with the truth. It always protects, always trusts, always hopes, always perseveres.

1 CORINTHIANS 13:4–7 (NIV)

I give you a new commandment: that you should love one another. Just as I have loved you, so you too should love one another.

JOHN 13:34

Above all things have intense and unfailing love for one another, for love covers a multitude of sins [forgives and disregards the offenses of others].

1 PETER 4:8

But I tell you, Love your enemies and pray for those who persecute you.

MATTHEW 5:44

Beloved, let us love one another, for love is (springs) from God; and he who loves [his fellowmen] is begotten (born) of God and is coming [progressively] to know and understand God [to perceive and recognize and get a better and clearer knowledge of Him]. He who does not love has not become acquainted with God [does not and never did know Him], for God is love.

1 JOHN 4:7–8

Let everything you do be done in love (true love to God and man as inspired by God's love for us).

1 CORINTHIANS 16:14

WAITING on GOD

But if we hope for what is still unseen by us, we wait for it with patience and composure.

ROMANS 8:25

And let us not lose heart and grow weary and faint in acting nobly and doing right, for in due time and at the appointed season we shall reap, if we do not loosen and relax our courage and faint.

GALATIANS 6:9

I wait for the Lord,
my whole being waits,
and in his word I put
my hope.

PSALM 130:5 (NIV)

Be still and rest in the Lord; wait for Him and patiently lean yourself upon Him; fret not yourself because of him who prospers in his way, because of the man who brings wicked devices to pass.

PSALM 37:7

Do not be anxious about anything, but in every situation, by prayer and petition, with thanksgiving, present your requests to God. And the peace of God, which transcends all understanding, will guard your hearts and your minds in Christ Jesus.

PHILIPPIANS 4:6–7 (NIV)

In the multitude of my [anxious] thoughts within me, Your comforts cheer and delight my soul!

PSALM 94:19

He has made everything beautiful in its time. He has also set eternity in the human heart; yet no one can fathom what God has done from beginning to end.

ECCLESIASTES 3:11 (NIV)

BELIEVING God & His WORD

But without faith it is impossible to please and be satisfactory to Him. For whoever would come near to God must [necessarily] believe that God exists and that He is the rewarder of those who earnestly and diligently seek Him [out].

HEBREWS 11:6

For we walk by faith [we regulate our lives and conduct ourselves by our conviction or belief respecting man's relationship to God and divine things, with trust and holy fervor; thus we walk] not by sight or appearance.

2 CORINTHIANS 5:7

Every Scripture is God–breathed (given by His inspiration) and profitable for instruction, for reproof and conviction of sin, for correction of error and discipline in obedience, [and] for training in righteousness (in holy living, in conformity to God's will in thought, purpose, and action).

2 TIMOTHY 3:16

Every word of God is tried and purified; He is a shield to those who trust and take refuge in Him. Add not to His words, lest He reprove you, and you be found a liar.

PROVERBS 30:5–6

How sweet are Your words to my taste, sweeter than honey to my mouth!

PSALM 119:103

It is the Spirit Who gives life [He is the Life-giver]; the flesh conveys no benefit whatever [there is no profit in it]. The words (truths) that I have been speaking to you are spirit and life.

JOHN 6:63

So faith comes by hearing [what is told], and what is heard comes by the preaching [of the message that came from the lips] of Christ (the Messiah Himself).

ROMANS 10:17

The POWER of your WORDS

Death and life are in the power of the tongue, and they who indulge in it shall eat the fruit of it [for death or life].

PROVERBS 18:21

The mind of the [uncompromisingly] righteous studies how to answer, but the mouth of the wicked pours out evil things.

PROVERBS 15:28

The words of a wise man's mouth are gracious and win him favor, but the lips of a fool consume him.

ECCLESIASTES 10:12

Understand [this], my beloved brethren. Let every man be quick to hear [a ready listener], slow to speak, slow to take offense and to get angry.

JAMES 1:19

A soft answer
turns away wrath,
but grievous words
stir up anger.

PROVERBS 15:1

Let no foul or polluting language, nor evil word nor unwholesome or worthless talk [ever] come out of your mouth, but only such [speech] as is good and beneficial to the spiritual progress of others, as is fitting to the need and the occasion, that it may be a blessing and give grace (God's favor) to those who hear it.

EPHESIANS 4:29

Let the words of my mouth and the meditation of my heart be acceptable in Your sight, O Lord, my [firm, impenetrable] Rock and my Redeemer.

PSALM 19:14

MENDING
a broken
HEART

He heals the brokenhearted and binds up their wounds [curing their pains and their sorrows].

PSALM 147:3

Casting the whole of your care [all your anxieties, all your worries, all your concerns, once and for all] on Him, for He cares for you affectionately and cares about you watchfully.

1 PETER 5:7

Cast your burden on the Lord [releasing the weight of it] and He will sustain you; He will never allow the [consistently] righteous to be moved (made to slip, fall, or fail).

PSALM 55:22

God is our Refuge and Strength [mighty and impenetrable to temptation], a very present and well-proved help in trouble.

PSALM 46:1

Praise be to the God and Father of our Lord Jesus Christ, the Father of compassion and the God of all comfort, who comforts us in all our troubles, so that we can comfort those in any trouble with the comfort we ourselves receive from God.

2 CORINTHIANS 1:3–4 (NIV)

Blessed and enviably happy [with a happiness produced by the experience of God's favor and especially conditioned by the revelation of His matchless grace] are those who mourn, for they shall be comforted!

MATTHEW 5:4

Come to Me, all you who labor and are heavy-laden and over-burdened, and I will cause you to rest. [I will ease and relieve and refresh your souls.]

MATTHEW 11:28

FINDING HOPE

Now may our Lord Jesus Christ Himself and God our Father, Who loved us and gave us everlasting consolation and encouragement and well–founded hope through [His] grace (unmerited favor), comfort and encourage your hearts and strengthen them [make them stead–fast and keep them unswerving] in every good work and word.

2 THESSALONIANS 2:16–17

May the God of your hope so fill you with all joy and peace in believing [through the experience of your faith] that by the power of the Holy Spirit you may abound and be overflowing (bubbling over) with hope.

ROMANS 15:13

The hope of the [uncompromisingly] righteous (the upright, in right standing with God) is gladness, but the expectation of the wicked (those who are out of harmony with God) comes to nothing.

PROVERBS 10:28

But those who wait for the Lord [who expect, look for, and hope in Him] shall change and renew their strength and power; they shall lift their wings and mount up [close to God] as eagles [mount up to the sun]; they shall run and not be weary, they shall walk and not faint or become tired.

ISAIAH 40:31

[What, what would have become of me] had I not believed that I would see the Lord's goodness in the land of the living! Wait and hope for and expect the Lord; be brave and of good courage and let your heart be stout and enduring. Yes, wait for and hope for and expect the Lord.

PSALM 27:13-14

But this I recall and therefore have I hope and expectation: It is because of the Lord's mercy and loving-kindness that we are not consumed, because His [tender] compassions fail not. They are new every morning; great and abundant is Your stability and faithfulness.

LAMENTATIONS 3:21-23

The Lord is good, a Strength and Stronghold in the day of trouble; He knows (recognizes, has knowledge of, and understands) those who take refuge and trust in Him.

NAHUM 1:7

LETTING GO of the PAST

For I know the thoughts and plans that I have for you, says the Lord, thoughts and plans for welfare and peace and not for evil, to give you hope in your final outcome.

JEREMIAH 29:11

Therefore if any person is [ingrafted] in Christ (the Messiah) he is a new creation (a new creature altogether); the old [previous moral and spiritual condition] has passed away. Behold, the fresh and new has come!

2 CORINTHIANS 5:17

Be gentle and forbearing with one another and, if one has a difference (a grievance or complaint) against another, readily pardoning each other; even as the Lord has [freely] forgiven you, so much you also [forgive].

COLOSSIANS 3:13

If we [freely] admit that we have sinned and confess our sins, He is faithful and just (true to His own nature and promises) and will forgive our sins [dismiss our lawlessness] and [continuously] cleanse us from all unrighteousness [everything not in conformity to His will in purpose, thought, and action].

1 JOHN 1:9

He has not dealt with us after our sins nor rewarded us according to our iniquities. For as the heavens are high above the earth, so great are His mercy and loving-kindness toward those who reverently and worshipfully fear Him. As far as the east is from the west, so far has He removed our transgressions from us.

PSALM 103:10-12

WALKING in PEACE

And let the peace (soul harmony which comes) from Christ rule (act as umpire continually) in your hearts [deciding and settling with finality all questions that arise in your minds, in that peaceful state] to which as [members of Christ's] one body you were also called [to live]. And be thankful (appreciative), [giving praise to God always].

COLOSSIANS 3:15

It is God who arms me with strength and keeps my way secure. He makes my feet like the feet of a deer; he causes me to stand on the heights. He trains my hands for battle; my arms can bend a bow of bronze. You make your saving help my shield, and your right hand sustains me; your help has made me great. You provide a broad path for my feet, so that my ankles do not give way.

PSALM 18:32–36 (NIV)

Peace I leave with you; My [own] peace I now give and bequeath to you. Not as the world gives do I give to you. Do not let your hearts be troubled, neither let them be afraid. [Stop allowing yourselves to be agitated and disturbed; and do not permit yourselves to be fearful and intimidated and cowardly and unsettled.]

JOHN 14:27

The Lord will give [unyielding and impenetrable] strength to His people; the Lord will bless His people with peace.

PSALM 29:11

Now may the Lord of peace Himself grant you His peace (the peace of His kingdom) at all times and in all ways [under all circumstances and conditions, whatever comes]. The Lord [be] with you all.

2 THESSALONIANS 3:16

The Lord is my Shepherd [to feed, guide, and shield me], I shall not lack. He makes me lie down in [fresh, tender] green pastures; He leads me beside the still and restful waters. He refreshes and restores my life (my self); He leads me in the paths of righteousness [uprightness and right standing with Him—not for my earning it, but] for His name's sake.

PSALM 23:1–3

The Lord lift up His [approving] countenance upon you and give you peace (tranquility of heart and life continually).

NUMBERS 6:26

JOYCE MEYER MINISTRIES
Sharing Christ – Loving People

Joyce Meyer Ministries is called to share the Gospel and extend the love of Christ. Through media we teach people how to apply biblical truth to every aspect of their lives and encourage God's people to serve the world around them. Through our missions arm, *Hand of Hope*, we provide global humanitarian aid, feed the hungry, clothe the poor, minister to the elderly, widows and orphans, visit prisoners and reach out to people of all ages and in all walks of life. *Joyce Meyer Ministries* is built on a foundation of faith, integrity and dedicated supporters who share this call.

For more information about *Joyce Meyer Ministries*, please visit joycemeyer.org or call (800) 727–9673. Outside the U.S. call (636) 349–0303.

Joyce Meyer Ministries • P.O. Box 655 • Fenton, MO 63026 USA • joycemeyer.org

 facebook.com/joycemeyerministries @joycemeyer